W9-BWU-578

Wonders of Nature
Caves

Dana Meachen Rau

Marshall Cavendish
Benchmark
New York

2

You cannot see if you are deep inside a dark cave. You cannot feel wind or other weather. The only sound might be water dripping on the cave floor.

A cave is a large *hollow* space inside a cliff or mountain. This empty space can be the size of a room!

Caves can have many rooms with *tunnels* from one to another. The rooms and tunnels of Mammoth Cave in Kentucky cover more than 350 miles.

Very big caves are called *caverns*. Carlsbad Caverns in New Mexico is one of the largest caves. One of the caverns is called the "Big Room." The "Big Room" is longer than five football fields.

Caves form over thousands of years. Most caves are made of a rock called *limestone*. Water flows into cracks in the limestone. The cracks get bigger.

The water wears away the rock. It makes bigger spaces in the rock.

The water carves out the rooms and tunnels of the cave.

Caves are often *damp* and wet. That is because many caves still have water inside. Some caves have lakes or even waterfalls.

The ceilings of some caves
look like they are covered
with icicles.

The floors of some caves have lumpy towers. These objects are made by dripping water.

Water mixes with materials in the rock called *minerals*. The water drips down and gets hard. It hangs from the ceiling or makes a tower on the floor.

Not many plants grow in caves. Most plants need sun to grow. Some green plants grow near the opening of a cave. Only plants like mushrooms can grow in a dark cave.

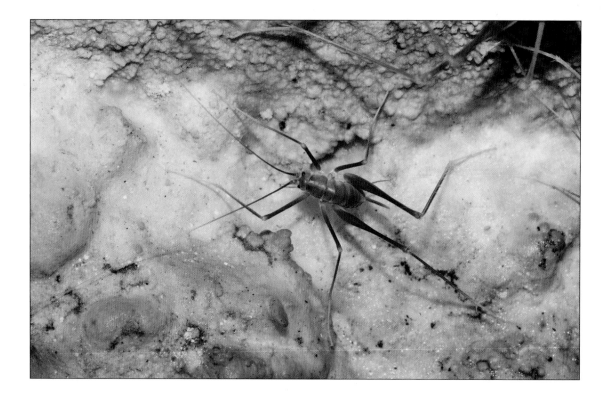

Many animals use caves
for *shelter*. Bears, mice, and
crickets live in caves.

They sleep in the cave. They leave the cave to find food.

Some bats sleep in caves
during the day. They live
in groups called *colonies*.

They hang upside down from the ceiling. They fly out at night to eat insects.

Some animals never leave the cave. They have grown used to living without light. Some of these animals do not even have eyes. They use other senses to know what is happening in the dark.

26

We know people lived in caves long ago. They left pictures behind on the cave walls. They drew pictures of the animals they hunted.

Some people like to explore caves. They have ropes to help them climb rocks. They wear hard hats with lights to help them see in the dark.

Challenge Words

caverns (KAV-uhrns)—Very large caves.

colonies (KAHL-uh-nees)—Groups of animals living together.

damp (DAMP)—A little wet.

hollow (HOL-oh)—Having an empty space on the inside.

limestone (LIME-stohn)—A soft kind of rock.

minerals (MIN-uhr-uhls)—Solid materials that are formed in the earth. Salt is a mineral.

shelter (SHEL-tuhr)—A safe place away from weather or danger.

tunnels (TUN-uhls)—Underground passages.

Index

Page numbers in **boldface** are illustrations.

With thanks to Nanci Vargus, Ed.D., and Beth Walker Gambro, reading consultants

Marshall Cavendish Benchmark
99 White Plains Road
Tarrytown, New York 10591-9001
www.marshallcavendish.us

Library of Congress Cataloging-in-Publication Data

Rau, Dana Meachen, 1971–
Caves / by Dana Meachen Rau.
p. cm. — (Bookworms. Wonders of nature)
Summary: "Provides a basic introduction to caves,
including geographical information and plant and animal life"—Provided by publisher.
Includes index.
ISBN 978-0-7614-2665-3
1. Cave ecology—Juvenile literature. 2. Caves—Juvenile literature. I. Title. II. Series.
QH541.5.C3R38 2007
577.5'84—dc22
2006038634

Editor: Christina Gardeski
Publisher: Michelle Bisson
Designer: Virginia Pope
Art Director: Anahid Hamparian

Photo Research by Anne Burns Images

Cover Photo by *Corbis*/Richard T. Nowitz

The photographs in this book are used with permission and through the courtesy of:
Peter Arnold: pp. 1, 14, 15 Fritz Polking; p. 2 Ron Giling; p. 11 BIOS/Denis Bringard.
Photo Researchers: pp. 4, 5, 20 Adam Jones; p. 21 William Ervin; p. 25 Dante Fenolio; p. 26 J.M. Labat.
Corbis: p. 7 Rainer Hackenberg/zefa; p. 8 Roger de la Harpe; p. 10 Michael Rose/Frank Lane Picture Agency;
p. 13 Macduff Everton; p. 17 Leo Batten/Frank Lane Picture Agency; p. 18 George Steinmetz;
pp. 22, 23 Eric & David Hosking; p. 29 Tim Wright.

Printed in Malaysia
1 3 5 6 4 2